Soul Ownership

Ryan Steinbeck is the author of nine previous collections of poetry:

Winter Solstice And What Follows -	2014
Sets In The West -	2014
Rises In The East -	2014
Tales Of A Stone Mason -	2013
Inside The Heart -	2011
One House Left Standing -	2009
Hurricane Catherine -	2007
Upper Level Disturbance -	2005
From Darkness Into Light -	2004

Soul Ownership

Ryan Fredric Steinbeck

Edited by Cynthia Steinbeck
Cover design by Michael R. Steinbeck

Published by Ryan Fredric Steinbeck
2016

Copyright © 2016 by Ryan Fredric Steinbeck

All rights reserved. This book or any portion thereof may not be reproduced or used in any manner whatsoever without the express written permission of the publisher except for the use of brief quotations in a book review or scholarly journal.

ISBN: 978-0-578-17835-6

Steinbeck Publications
Chesterton, Indiana 46304

First Printing 2016

Ordering Information:

Special discounts are available on quantity purchases by corporations, associations, educators, and others. For details, contact the publisher.

U.S. trade bookstores and wholesalers: Please contact Ryan Fredric Steinbeck: email ryan@ryanfsteinbeck.com

Dedications

To my wife, Cindy for encouragement, support and putting up with my ramblings. To Mike Steinbeck for innovation, and putting up with my pestering.
Without your support, help, and patience, I would not be where I am today.

Contents

Soul Ownership 1
Something Big Is Happening Today 2
Out Of The Gate 3
Wonder 4
Thoughts And Memories of This Region 5
Glimpse (Light Of Dawn) 7
Punto De Reunion 8
Lighthouse Off The Coast 10
Elegy For Brussels 12
One Way Mirror 13
Dark Road 14
Why, How, May, If, Can, Will 15
Apparition Over Franklin Drive 16
Killing Kind 17
Broken Pencils 18
Flaws 20
Platform One 21
When Love Is All We Have Left 22
Shift In Consciousness 23
Joy 24
Everyone Needs A Hug 25
Golden Heart 26
Burning Bridge 27
The Curious Turtle 28
Origins Of This Day 29

Stand Up Special 30
The Simple Life Of Roy 31
Used To Be 32
Reincarnated As Leaves 33
Observe 34
Beautiful Horizon 35
Still, Calm The River 36
Today Is The Day 37
Understood 38
To All 39
Reasons 40
Ten Years 41
Only Good Things 42
I Wouldn't Have It Any Other Way 43

Acknowledgements:

I would like to thank my teachers and mentors. I wouldn't be here without you. Thank you friends and family for your patience, guidance, and stories you may not realize you provide me on a daily basis.

"It is good to have an end to journey toward; but it is the journey that matters in the end."
— **Ursula K. Le Guin**

Soul Ownership

Quiet is the violin of sunrise,
inaudible to my rising consciousness.
As the book of day opens,
it repairs the piers and battered piles of my soul.

Fossils of failure are entombed.
Attention span vagrants are detained.
Ancient truths are revealed,
as I go back to using my hands.

A vision from the first perception,
drawing diagrams of ghosts.
I exhume the wisdom of mystics:
"Don't lie down on command,
pick gold from the corruption tree,
teach what you haven't learned,
give what you don't own,
or take what you haven't earned.
Are you meant to be led by your nose?
What percentage of you is you?"

Time becomes a tool,
seeds in autumn,
growth in spring.
I become what I am,
a citizen of the world,
my thoughts shape my politics,
I turn away these beggars and peddlers,
no longer should I bargain
for a soul I already own.

Something Big Is Happening Today

I step into remnants of daylight,
thought-forms of an ancient pharaoh belief.
Peace alleviates the world's weight.
The blinding beacons of ideologies have temporarily dimmed.
I thought evil was winning today,
until I crossed desolate streets.
In a rocky canvas once a river bed,
water emerges from dry soil cracks,
flowers victoriously rise from decay.
Something big is happening today.

Converted, I surrender,
to the fog of transformation.
My theme evolves from the middle ages of gratitude.
A temple to the sun,
before my own Council of Trent,
reforming my corrupted nature.
I see through the playful disguise,
as woods give way to light,
as the epiphany of the new world rises to power.
I'm fortunate to witness this maze of untamed surroundings,
to which everything bows and accedes,
to a fleeting manifestation of transcendence on display.
Something big is happening today.

Out Of The Gate

Under the loft,
born and raised in the hay.
At the moonlight, I gaze.
A distant mountain skyline calls.

On these pastures, inside these fences,
under saddles, blinders, and riding crops,
defeat waits for me.

Every third Wednesday,
they exit through the meadow,
on their high horse,
picking apples in the orchard,
unhurried is their gait.
I know my day is today.

My vantage from the barn door,
I cross the line into sunlight.
My trot turns to a canter, then a gallop.
They unlock the steel barrier,
I advance to a sprint,
my leap clears their frames,
my airstream disrupts their motion.
I no longer acknowledge their commands.
Mountains are approaching,
I've no intent to refrain.

The measure of a tiny mind,
is the need for control.
Conveyance is now an inconvenience.
I'm no longer tied to their fate,
no more carrying their weight,
I'm out of the gate.

Wonder

There's beauty in altitude,
elements of awareness.
A falling sensation,
I dive into exploration,
through the world of clouds,
over uneven skies,
the thrill of the ride,
like a statue coming to life,
from a disembodied soul.
A rediscovery before time corrodes me.

I wonder if I can change what is unchangeable.
I wonder if I could be your super power,
if you'll survive my lack of sanity.
I wonder if I'll remember my life in heaven.
I wonder if I've missed my opportunity.
I wonder about an alternate set of tracks,
if the moon and tide will lead me back.
I wonder if I get here by overthinking.

As the world plays oppressor,
there's fear of time's appetite
Wonder is therapy,
the antidote,
a remedy.
A ceremonial initiation,
into the greatest of displays,
as it discovers you,
repairs you,
and gives meaning to your passage.

Thoughts And Memories of This Region

We are crossing patterns.
From this dune I look across the lake.
I am one with new sunrise,
as birds play on the rocky beach.
Acetylene from steel mills carries heavy in cold morning air.
This view never tires.

We are drifters;
This body of water, this river, our county borders,
of these times and tracks with trains on wires.
Within this quiet settlement,
I'm surrounded by everyone and everything I've ever known.

One hundred and fifty years.
An oversight, a historical lapse,
from a night shift without radio,
a town without community,
to the inter-urban train whistle,
conceding the shift from farms to factories.

My grandfather spoke of hardship,
growing up mean and strong,
bailing hay and shoveling coal
for two dollars a day,

My grandmother lifted her eyes from her victory garden
as her elders arrived on horse and buggy,
with homemade dairy from Jackson Center.
A promise delivered every week.

In my time I've missed what used to be;
The picnics and playgrounds,
the smallness of childhood,
before invaders from the north.

Still, with family and familiarity,
positioned near and far enough from the great city,
these amazing sands of safeguarded lands,
there must be something here.
Every time I've had the opportunity to leave,
I've chosen to stay.

Glimpse (Light Of Dawn)

I was an early explorer to this area.
I dreamt of an inaccessible mountain.
I ascended to the southeast edge of the south face,
enduring glacier climbs and gullies,
then layers upon layers of snow.
That was when I caught a glimpse of sunrise.
The auburn rocks reflected the diverging rays through ice,
as if flames were lighting the way.
I wanted to live in that moment forever,
but I knew I couldn't stay.

A rift valley pulls away continental plates.
I'm immersed in groundwater reserves.
The marine environment spills its secrets,
revealing a map of historical formations.
I catch a glimpse of the world before,
from the shoals to the undersea range.
I dig in for the odyssey of survival,
but know in due course it will change.

I once thought I was distinguished.
I let myself be ruined.
I hadn't realized my suffering,
was vital to enlightenment.
The separation and essential death of me,
was the suspended weightlessness
that can only arise when you've become something more,
yet something less all the same.
In that void between existence,
I was momentarily complete.
That was when I caught a brief glimpse of love.
It was everything I'd imagined it would be.

Punto De Reunion

Scarce becomes the air.
Sometimes I look behind me,
as I ascend this dusty mountain switchback
until it disappears in billows.
I wrestle with the Asturias winds.
The Cantabrian peaks are rockets in the sky.
The only sound is silence between footsteps.
Skilled I am at this ascent,
at putting distance between us.
A spoof of our sincerest times
plays out over the limestone landscape.

I've been overburdened and underwhelmed,
long searching of the hum of the universe.
I sense the brightest point in the sky,
the exact place where the weight shifts,
the imagery and consciousness,
symbols of meaning and importance,
Yahweh and the floating tree,
essays from the gods of the world,
a showcase of our diminutive nature.

Higher and higher,
the Torre De Cerredo in sight.
Up here I'm anonymous,
the trees don't know me.
I'm the fear in the voice of the climb,
of those at the foothills.

Into thin air,
out of nowhere,
you reveal your truths,
you forgive the missteps.
I came up here to release these demons,
they have been released.

On my way down,
we are strangers in passing.
We both knew this was necessary,
though the timing's unprecedented.
It speaks to the need for closure,
this unplanned reunion.
I return to common ground,
knowing we can both put it behind us now.

Lighthouse Off The Coast

Our wreckage was discovered the other day,
after the decree I received
lead me through impossible terrain.
It was an unmarked plot on the map,
I suspect this was your doing.

The winch fights and twists,
pulling it to shore.
I haven't seen that old body style in forever.

The blustery cold.
The wind burned hands and faces
as they sift through broken plans.
Eventually I'm given the all clear.
I overanalyze every piece
until I forget why I'm here.
Just another flaw in my blueprint.

You were right all along,
to rise from this,
I'm a ship drawn to sinking,
a mind drawn to overthinking.
These days you're off the grid,
beneath soft light in a quiet town,
where congregations avoid your spaces.

Every now and then,
there's a gust from your warm coordinates.
I long to rebuild our exhibition of artifacts,
then exchange this old currency for new.
I know this was never the going rate,
I know I would've left you stranded
in the village time abandoned.

If you need a whisper of truth,
or a haunting by the ghost of our short story
to reassure your decision,
you can look in my direction.
I'll always be your lighthouse off the coast.

Elegy For Brussels

Here I am waiting for a time,
when my memory didn't cry,
when my conscience didn't stall in the rain.

I was raised on a fable of peace,
an old fashioned belief,
something I still hold onto.

I'm the curious adventurer,
the gatherer and optimist.
I'm not out to win the hand of the devil
that rattles the skeleton of the earth,
or builds a foundation of fear.

You cannot change who I am, who we are.
We'll rebuild a reckless faith that has crumbled.
Our strength will not diminish with this endeavour.
I've never become a beast to kill the beast,
nor will I ever.

One Way Mirror

A story began unfolding,
as you went your own way,
with answers in search of questions.
Now careless with blame,
a changed name,
you ignore the enemy of time,
the perimeter of patience is frayed.
Maybe this is a permanent fissure.

We bury our sorrow in efforts of courtesy,
requesting a consensus on conceptual boundaries,
an acknowledgement of all we've given you.
Essays on your lack of forgiveness,
are now eroding excuses.

You said to love is to be underestimated,
to love is to be incarcerated,
to love is to be questioned,
to love is to play victim,
to love is to remain in isolation,
our love manifests as guilt,
love is a one way mirror shattered by a high pitched scream,
love is a saltwater fish in a freshwater stream,
Did you mean what you said?

Your submission is glacial in pace.
Maybe we don't deserve each other.
Maybe this dark divide will persist.
A stony impasse looms a short distance ahead.
When we appear before you
in a vision beyond our last day,
will we see the truth through lies?
Will we understand what we did?

Dark Road

I had great plans
to prevent a demise,
every step to that end,
still an end has beckoned.

Electrical and chemical,
every movement is stone on grinding stone.
A dark turn on a poorly lit walk,
I'm uplinked with the turning earth,
running toward a conclusion.
I may never see the dawns and sunsets,
or evergreens of legend.

Mystery is the new certainty.
Threats to my balance and maintenance
increase in weight.
My arms shake under the shift.
Lesions through moral fibers
never heal or expand.

With awareness of what I've become,
I prepare a defense
for my lack of radiance,
desolation is imminent.
They say there's reason for celebration,
reason to fear.

Under the umbrella of nightfall,
artificial lights provide ineffective guidance
to the other side,
where I am engulfed in prehistoric black.
This sector of the dark road
is the part I must walk alone.
Though I'm determined to make it back.

Why, How, May, If, Can, Will

I know that seeing is not believing
until subtleties are detonated.
Every moment becomes critical
after x-rays and blueprints deceive.

I've punished words like "why" and "how,"
after memorizing disloyalty.
In the empty auditorium of senses,
promises and plans no longer resonate.

He fights a cruelty undeserved,
in the breadth of a skeletal frame,
harmonious for so long,
wants to be again.

I find myself using words like "may" and "if."
as I study the enemy within.
There's a depth of focus required for hope,
essential to starting over.
The only therapy appears to be faith.

Still, as he stands here before me,
I observe an unfailing glimmer inside.
It's progress to arrive here,
to speak the words "can" and "will."

Apparition Over Franklin Drive

This unplanned detour,
on a path I'd been avoiding.
I passed by where I last saw you,
where we said goodbye,
my heart heavy and sinking.
I thought I'd escaped mostly unscathed,
but the fog ahead was unusual,
soft grey and piercing blue,
the ghost of you I passed through.

One inhale and all outside was in my lungs.
Then it traveled,
projecting memories in my head.
I relived all my excuses.

Later in the evening,
I spoke about the apparition over Franklin Drive.
I'm not sure she believed me.
That night I dreamt about my life of alibis.
So much for attempting to remain in hiding.

The next day like withdrawal,
a peaceful exhale.
I watched you disperse as silver crystals
over the place where you lived.
Calm replaced the unrest I sensed before.
I realized you were lingering out on that drive,
waiting for me to be your carrier.
You just wanted to return home.

Killing Kind

In a wave of commotion,
a trail of traces concludes.
in the absence of efficiency and inefficiency,
the fulcrum ruptures.

I received a late afternoon call,
requesting my reclamation,
I've yet to make a mark
in the heart of it all.

I am in the winter.
Whether midsummer or spring,
I am in the winter.
Long in wait for irrigation,
promised but not delivered.
Broken vows were not the intent,
I apologize for leaving it this way.

At one time, maybe fear,
I don't remember.
I've been working on accepting my design.
Facing what I know to be fact,
I step out from the shadow of lies,
I'm blanketed in ultraviolet light,
exposing my transparency.
Scars and unseen violence revealed,
and they're the killing kind.

Aftershocks of goodwill may heal.
Memories will reverberate,
as long as memories sustain.
I'm good with taking the long way to heaven,
as long as some evidence remains,
as long as these thoughts travel well,
as long as I see you there someday.

Broken Pencils

You came up in conversation today.
I, in a different sequence,
had to elaborate.
When we visit, when I see you,
I see the path I refused,
what I could've become.
I never let my observance become behavior,
or my behavior become habit.

We fought every step.
You were my hope and rage.
I hadn't realized all the monsters
I tried to avoid,
had manifested themselves as barricades.

My conviction is worn thin,
like the clothes in my paper bag.
I'm not as strong as I claim.
If you could tell me you cared just once,
then all may not be lost.

I don't remember if I told you,
when I gathered broken pencils on the playground,
to keep them secure and safe,
so they wouldn't have to be alone.
I valued their damaged state.
We were one in the same.

I deferred from your democracy,
I took the highway under the moon and stars.
I bypassed your condemned mind.
I refused to be your casualty,
you blamed for your choices.

I've moved beyond unanswered echoes.
I said goodbye to the old gin soaked goat.
The sun rises differently here.
The space between thoughts speaks to me,
building on a ceasefire that declares I belong,
as do the faces smiling back at me.
I purge memories of everything familiar,
I blame you and forgive you,
then let all of it go.

Flaws

These voices come from an empty well.
They come from a place of poisoned streams,
from a place that doesn't know reason,
from a place the knows no peace.

Towers of bias without infrastructure,
they're made in a place that doesn't know irony,
in a cavern with hollow chambers.
from a rebuttal that knows no argument,

As a child I was told:
"Before you run your mouth,
take a look at yourself,
and a good look around,
your flaws may run just as deep,
just as wide as the river obliviousness,
you claim to be crossing."

"Be sure to bring some belongings.
You may not return from the other side.
Excavated skeletons are exposed on the banks.
You may come to find
they were buried alongside your own."

I question the ownership of these voices,
though my judgement is one of my flaws,
so I burn them in a shallow pit,
my cast iron certainty along with it.

Platform One

At ground level below the station,
I watch as a crowd assembles.
Time is a high speed train behind schedule,
the changing seasons roar by.
I blink and miss everything I hoped to feel.

I barely saw your face in lowlight,
but made out your expression of sorrow,
I figured it out long before you told me.

My view finder memory sifts through your photos.
I know there was a time when you smiled,
it may have been a distorted dream,
the evidence escapes me.

I watched you struggle to climb
the broken stairs of platform one,
just before you boarded.
I tried to put the rain back in the clouds,
it seems I fall short on miracles every time.

Across the city,
the morning light through broken stained glass.
A flash of blinding brilliance,
off the cross, onto the wall,
your image with my eyes closed.
Wind carries your whisper,
telling me to stop the worry,
your suffering has ended.

On the last of these days,
I roll into the sky and redirect jet streams.
For a moment I hold back the rain,
so to wish for second chances,
before I inevitably accept this day.
But my darling what do I wear,
when the train takes you away?

When Love Is All We Have Left

Always eternal and fleeting,
the waters of resolution are shallow.
Wading into the river,
buying into the current,
disturbing the past,
disrupting the habitat.
To drag the riverbed,
would only disperse sediment like smoke.

Wake up on the morning side
in a scattered mind out of reason,
a boundary line crossed,
in a wasteland of moral stalemates.

A child forced to come of age,
may never pull back the frame,
to see the decomposing ideology.
While he clutches the wrong rope,
the treasures of his life are lost in floodplains

We prepare a treaty of benevolence,
to observe a revolution that may follow.
Maybe we'll finally know peace,
when love is all we have left.

Shift In Consciousness

These strains in your life's cargo hold,
your knees buckle under loads of assertions,
when you were too young to know consequences,
or promises you made to yourself.

On your heels,
absorbing the best punches.
It becomes familiar,
it begets comfort.

Command and control,
is there for the taking.
It only requires a changing mind,
a simple shift in consciousness.

Joy

There is no secret passage.
The melody of the world cannot steal this voice,
it's rightfully mine
to meld into shape.

When I share, it multiplies.
It's not practical and shouldn't be.
It's dormant if concealed,
but never dies.

Contemplate it,
live for it,
live in it,
give and receive it.
Don't over think it.
Joy is always there
waiting to be celebrated.

Everyone Needs A Hug

Everyone vacates from their ideologies sometimes.
Pride is a bitter pill to swallow.
After explosive words,
an embrace can absorb the violence.
Silence is an adequate last verse.

With a specific method of operation,
they point a finger in my direction
for running over the cats tail.
It's difficult to blame the accuser,
when the past has a way of biting your ankles.

Once a swindler,
I bought my soul off a bargain tree,
an exchange in a back alley,
overpriced, its value abruptly declined,
eventually it cost me.

The spirit evolves.
The serenade of disgrace fades,
like the coda of an 80's song.
I will no longer take credit for the call of this bird.
I'm clearing space to write my own verse.
I will create a new beginning,
I will not be conceding to the same end.

Golden Heart

He said he had the words
to change the world.
A guarded secret
in a distant land,
inside the archives of his mind.

He held in his hand
a once broken heart,
mended with ages of fruition.

The era of misery settled upon them,
rivaled only by their prophecy,
where they gained control of hostility.
Emotional demonstrations
filled the seven seas with elemental songs.

As he emerged from impartiality,
he held in his hand
the golden heart,
responsible for the stars.

In one shade of love,
they're continents apart,
divided by lunar impulses,
by cataclysms of regret.

He remains adrift,
between static of sapphire and ashen,
partially living his life.
He evolves and opens his eyes,
breathing in the salty undercurrent,
until the undertow gives him back.
With love in every direction,
he tames hereditary fear.
With this noble golden heart,
once divisive,
it now begins to unite.

Burning Bridge

This is the end.
My era of inconsequence
is a sigh of relief,
there will be more to life.

My tenure comes down to some boxes,
some final farewells,
promises to stay in touch.
I'm trading security for sanity,
before the replacement regime
disintegrates to shambles.
I was here before,
as witness to the worst decline in history.
A futile investment in younger currency,
with an exchange rate on steady decline,
when there are no traditionalists,
left to build a better vision.

I force the rusty handle open.
Shards of sunlight fill the hall.
In my room of optimism your words fall away,
I still have plenty to say.

I've followed,
fell in line,
I let you take everything,
bearing your mutated injustice.
Your straw broke the entire camel,
you are a haystack with no needle.
I gave my soul to this place,
you let it disintegrate.
I torched the memory of you,
the burning bridge behind me,
will decorate the arch of clouds,
while it forges a new trail,
that will light my way home.

The Curious Turtle

So many ways
between a rock and a hard place.
She'll try them all,
succeed at none.

The curious turtle observes,
she thinks outside her space,
as if she begs for knowledge
she knows she shouldn't have.

A soldier of resistance,
a genetic anomaly
looking to survive the odds.
Gentle, peaceful, delicate,
borderline indestructible.
With time on her side,
this curious turtle
is one for the ages.

Origins Of This Day

In fields where we laughed and played,
we learned to believe in each other.
It brings us to this day,
magnificence and procession,
rites and obligation.
An evolving institution,
restrictive to uninhibited within a matter of moments.
We're encircled by flowers and brilliant gardens,
as anticipation grows in heavy air.

This celebratory groundwork is prepared.
We stand looking one hundred miles ahead.
The gift is not just in symbols,
but a part of ourselves.

Chambers of time mark the memory.
We drift to the beginning:
The first look, laugh, and touch.
The origins of this day
bring us back to this moment.
To be engraved in our minds,
for all the days to follow.

Stand Up Special

You may think it's foolish,
but this stand up special is a rehashing,
a stony path to the ledge,
overlooking the synagogue.
The straits of my childhood flow beyond it,
the hills of my youth climb above it,
the fields of my ageing grow around it,
the palace of my eventual demise built beside it.
I'm a second hand story to the events unfolding.

To effortlessly lift out of purpose,
land in the first day of an idea,
in the first desert thirsty for growth,
long before the wrong turns,
before I interfered.

To become an institution
beneath sacred arches and towers,
to accomplish what no earthlings have before,
to feel received at a gathering,
neither fatigued nor overcrowded,
to stay within a limitless mural,
is a dream in a world of action without thought,
but it's a dream I will hold onto.

The Simple Life Of Roy

A quantifiable strategic impossibility,
a mathematical improbability,
superhumanly ordinary,
an implausibly gifted leader.

Articulating the right thought
at precisely the right time.
Defibrillating the pressure in the room
with a sixth sense of comedy.
An elder jester,
with a mast of underrated astuteness.
A travel wise companion,
with a hand-me-down conscience.
A sage and prospect
for future generations who discover his handbook.

Veiled in ancient mystery,
outdated but not obsolete.
It must be an absolute joy to experience,
the simple life of Roy.

Used To Be

Though I don't remember the passing autumns,
I often miss them.
I close the hatch and gather my possessions,
Soon after I discover a note to myself
about a sleep chamber and hyperspace.
I allude to ten years of travel.

In the time passed,
the travel log turned disgraceful.
I'm glad I don't remember me
before I fell asleep.
Bouncing off satellites,
anticipation of decent,
I pour blind faith into hope of arrival.

I wake without a compass or VOR,
with a familiar gravitational pull.
A recent feed says she's waiting,
somehow I'm still worth the wait.

To recognize my surroundings,
feels instant and eternal.
Satellites record my encounter with ether.
I notify the station I've returned.
The one who left would've cherished
being a spectacle for all to see,
but I'm not who I used to be.

Reincarnated As Leaves

I am a leaf.
Wind guided, I land in the stream.
Water is cold in my veins.

I see those before me trapped on the bend,
unable to circumvent the bank's shallow stagnate.
Maybe it's my wide margin,
or the curve of my blade,
I catch the right current,
I drift to the center.
I hope to join the inside passage
beyond raging rapids,
just before the calm.

The water befits me.
The channel evades a timestamp,
though I know my time is borrowed.

I'm a destined wanderer,
I have an end,
I feel my aging,
my phantom limb.

Everyone leaves.
My journey is solitary,
from source to mouth,
duration unspecified.
The objective is to stay afloat.
Maybe translation won't be so literal,
next time around.

Observe

These were my initial efforts,
my interludes,
as if I woke something else up,
in the sparing sky amid colors of timber.
Leaves plummet in spherical patterns,
one gracefully lands in my open hand,
others fall in peaceful cascades,
imprinting on wood platforms,
minor preparations for an approaching slumber.

I breathe in the silence of this frigid forest air.
If I play any part at all,
it's only to observe,
then leave it all alone.

Beautiful Horizon

It happens during my stray thoughts,
the universe comes into focus.
Crafted and distinctive,
they theorized it accidental,
to avoid the mundane.
In the framework of the unchanging,
there is always erratic change.

If this ends,
it will somehow remain,
from some point of view,
light years away.

An acquired friendship,
a tangible whole.
We're united in the need to know.
No wars exist on whether to allow it.

Every night ends the same,
we know just how it will go,
and still revel in the brilliance.
The axis turns,
the darkest of nights give way,
morning provides a hint of color,
as the picture develops.

All eyes turn,
as it refracts and reflects.
From the eastern fire,
I feel reborn.
It never fails to be new,
the beautiful horizon.

Still, Calm The River

A young girl,
relentlessly jumping off deep ends,
insists she knows how she'll feel
when erosion carves her face,
and the kids are older.

There's a river down the hill,
through the woods,
a short walk from her door.
The peaceful, migratory calm
is always in her mind.

Wrong she was
when his restlessness took form,
leaving empty chairs at the table,
empty prescriptions in need of filling.

The volcano inside awakens,
on a cold holiday morning.
The world she knows isn't ending,
but close
Still, calm the river.

She distances herself today,
beyond the opens fields.
Stillness is her motto.
The river is a magnet.
She tries to move past it,
but remains.
The constancy is reassuring this time of year,
as if it always has answers.

Roaring falls are behind.
The mouth leads to the deep, dark sea.
These truths will never be confined,
still, calm the river.

Today Is The Day

My historical record skips.
I'm losing track of my days.
They advertise innovation,
when what they want is repetition.
I'm not sure what made me slow down,
or translate the writing on the wall.
All I know is what I've seen from these blind loyalists.
If their soul was a house on fire,
they'd let it burn to the ground.

I've been accustomed for too long.
My hide's been strung out, stretched and beaten.
So long have I taken orders,
I don't recall another way.

Today is the day.
This is no longer a wish,
this is action.
I'm auctioning off my fear.
I'm exiting the crowded corridor,
of the revolving door,
to reshape the fortunes I've been destroying,
as the sun sets on this segment of my life.

It's time to speak my mind,
to explore the depths of my inspiration,
to apologize and make amends,
to return accumulating favors,
to forgive knowing I've also been guilty,
to hand out gratitude,
to love unreservedly,
to preserve my mental state,
before it secedes.

Today is the day to unchain my soul,
and give it life.

Understood

I paused my pace for moment,
to witness a shimmer of afternoon sun,
off the fiery courthouse bricks,
above the unscalable, overhanging slab.
In contradiction to a warning sound nearby,
my soul is resurrected by the sight,
like a devil raised from the ground.

Survival tactics are disseminated
from chambers of a heart repeatedly infiltrated.
Its walls and doors worn to inefficiency.
Recuperation has been sluggish.

Multiple climbs to the crest,
now comes the drought.
The warmth of day is healing.
The sum of me is decoded to modern language.
I hear voices around me,
a convergence of townspeople,
emerging from shadows for this day,
as my peace is made public.
I am closer than ever to being understood.

To All

First the cold, then the rain,
freezing in glacial basins,
melting in spring trenches,
an overstated, predictable pattern,
a work in progress.

Underlain in heavier substance,
a safety harbor,
with praiseworthy punishment,
for a darkened soul.
It's a feeling when no one's left.
Not a fear of loss,
but a fear of gain,
of reoccurrence.
The reminiscence of delusion,
coursing through veins.
Memories hide in segmented plumes,
by way of cracks in our linguistic tundra.
During the original freefall,
a challenge of redemption is accepted.
It's just a little miracle,
from those gone before,
as they remember us,
we remember them in turn,
while the mind rises and falls at night,
and substructures close for repair.
When what you are was made better
by who they were.
Say a prayer in your subconscious;
Rest in peace to them,
to all.

Reasons

Photographs long exposed the memory,
of moisture-laden clouds in mist,
a moonbow over tributary stillness.
It took years of confluence,
to appreciate this disparity.

In late afternoon blues
of an overused excuse,
I found my reason.
Me as adversity's architect,
combining potent chemicals
in a stream of doubt,
with my back against the fallout shelter.

Until an inside needs out,
to be carried and believed,
did I find something unconditional.
The contributor is a mainstay,
the beneficiary has been salvaged,
she will always be,
these are my reasons.

Ten Years

The edge of the floor and end of fear,
on and off each other's toes.
Faces in the dark,
swiftly they move,
looking away.
Absent exchanges,
hovering into crowds for dialogue,
evading a slower dance.

You're all I see across from me,
darkly lit your eyes glow.
Noise outside,
eternally low.
This freight train life we take it slow.
We know the music,
appreciate these customs,
but tend to break from the ordinary.
Ten years on,
your glow is still a part of me,
we remain the focus of our story.

Only Good Things

A memorial symphony
in the parting of ways.
I was given a moment,
I cherished it.

I made a wish,
it was granted.
I felt it new,
felt it aging,
felt it old,
when it was time, I knew.

I wouldn't trade the noise or the quiet,
nor deny any part was essential.
The angels in the architecture have a new design for me.
Whether denied or admitted,
I saw this day in the distance.

On my way
into the dawn of hindsight,
as I call to mind the memories,
my dream of you feels like contact.
I scour through the present and history.
I remember only good things.

I Wouldn't Have It Any Other Way

Today I remembered what it was like to be awake,
my footprints displayed in sequence.
My mind pulled from evaporitic deposits
of monotony's erosion,
where I witnessed an entire universe in a molecule.

The demons that tracked me over the sea
were ambushed over the skyway.
There's now room on my walls for mindless sculpture,
room on my shelves for conception and satire.
I am an open book that's closed to fear, violence, and hate.

With only a handful of words left,
I'd go back and begin again,
if I was promised to meet the same end.

If they say I've been grateful, true, and giving,
that my actions were honorable to my last day,
then I wouldn't have it any other way.

Notes on the Poems

Soul Ownership:
It's a constant struggle to stay grounded. It seems as if every company and everything wants a piece of you. Be careful what parts you give away.

Something Big Is Happening Today:
I wrote this on Christmas Day, 2015 during a walk down quiet, deserted streets and past the river. It was reassuring to know that on some days, important concepts remain bigger than us.

Glimpse (Light of Dawn):
When a friend loses someone dear, your heart breaks a little too.

Punto De Reunion:
The Cantabrian Mountains are in Northern Spain, its highest peak is the Torre De Cerredo, at 8,688 feet. I'm not really sure if the main character is reuniting with a ghost or with a past acquaintance in real form. Either way it allowed for progress.

Dark Road, Why, How, May, If Can, Will:
Cancer is a group of diseases characterized by uncontrolled growth and spread of abnormal cells. It's difficult to watch a good friend struggle through it. I remain forever optimistic.

Apparition Over Franklin Drive:
Sometimes ghosts of loved ones come back to haunt you.

Broken Pencils:
For my cousin.

Burning Bridge:
It's difficult to see a loved one suffer through a dead end situation. If and when it gets to that point, often you'll get the best light from a burning bridge.

Used To Be:
Who I am and who I was feels like completely different people who have very little in common.

Observe:
Pausing often to observe and appreciate the simple things is critical and rejuvenating to me.

Today Is The Day:
Accentuating the topic of the entire collection, the character decides to take control of his life and his soul.

I Wouldn't Have It Any Other way:
The goal is to be remembered as someone who lived a life with a predominate characteristic of integrity.

www.ingramcontent.com/pod-product-compliance
Lightning Source LLC
Chambersburg PA
CBHW031504040426
42444CB00007B/1206